JIM C WILSON

WILL I EVER GET TO MINSK?

HAPPENSTANCE

Acknowledgements:
Thanks to editors of the following publications, in which these poems,
or versions of them, first appeared.
• Magazines
*Acumen, Blithe Spirit, Chapman, East Lothian Life, Haiku Scotland,
New Writing Scotland, Northwords Now, Orbis, Poetry Scotland, , Radical
Scotland, Scotland on Sunday, still, The Dark Horse, The Herald, The
Journal of Stevenson Studies, The Red Wheelbarrow, The Scotsman.*
• Anthologies
Present Poets (National Museums of Scotland, 1998), *Present Poets
(2)* (NMS, 1999), *The Edinburgh Book of Scottish 20th-Century Poetry*
(Edinburgh University Press, 2005), *Skein of Geese*, (StAnza anthology,
2008),*Variations on a New Song*, (Scottish Poetry Library, 2000), *100
Favourite Scottish Poems*, (Luath, 2006), *100 Major Modern Poets* (Orbis
anthology, 1996).

By the same author:
Cellos in Hell, (Chapman, 1993)
Paper Run, (Mariscat, 2007)
Spalebone Days, (Kettillonia, 2002)
The Loutra Hotel, (Making Waves, 1988)
The Happy Land, (Ramsay Head, 1991).

Printed by The Dolphin Press
www.dolphinpress.co.uk

Published in 2012 by Happen*Stance*,
21 Hatton Green, Glenrothes, Fife KY7 4SD
nell@happenstancepress.com
www.happenstancepress.com

Orders:
Individual pamphlets £4.00 (includes UK P&P).
Please make cheques payable to Happen*Stance* or order
through PayPal in the website shop.

CONTENTS

For Mik,
for past and present students
of my 'Poetry in Practice' workshops
and
for everyone who has yet to travel
to Minsk

SUNDAY SCHOOL

They told us stories; we marvelled
at wee boys born bright with haloes
and babes that bounced in bulrush baskets,
hidden in riverside reeds.

More wondrous tales unfolded:
Noah navigated and Samson slew
while the Hebrews got fresh quails for lunch.
God's voice spake out from a burning bush.

And the tea-urn gleamed and steamed.
Its warm smell hung, heavy and slow,
with a promise of dusty floorboards
and the hell of hard benches for hours.

No fiery revelations; just cups of tea
and a Sunday expanse of wilderness.

THE TIME OF MY LIFE

As frost makes the grass grow more brittle
a thin hand closes round my heart.
There are places I shouldn't return to.

Cold linoleum glints in the moonlight.
Panic and emptiness wait in the hall
and frost makes the grass grow more brittle.

The doorbell clamours; the light goes out.
Thudding heartbeats echo in the kitchen.
There are places I shouldn't return to.

The wireless is stilled; the valves smell of dust.
Strange fists beat on the dark-varnished door
while frost makes the grass grow more brittle.

Grown-ups cry when they're scared and in pain
then they'll rage and curse through endless night
in the places I shouldn't return to.

I'll hang for what I'll do to you, she says.
I pick at the skin that covers my cocoa
while frost makes the grass grow more brittle;
there are places I shouldn't return to.

THE MEDICAL DICTIONARY

Will my ceiling burst into vengeful flame
if I lie, this light summer night, and read
the medical dictionary? Will my bed
become a storm-tossed raft, sucked down by guilt
and blame? Those rough-sketched ladies draw me in
to the thick musty pages, stiff with sin.

Cold nudes, emotionless, stand at their ease,
baring doctored parts, glimpses of disease.
Fingering the index, I probe for the facts
of life and lust. I look under *Nipples,*
Penis, Pudenda. But bags, tubes and gunge
are all I can find—and the cripples.

No fires high above or glow down below:
just warm muttering from a muffled wireless—
and that piercing thrust of dark remorse
as I let the book go, let it drop limply.
The handle of my bedroom door is turning;
will it be Mum, the bogeyman, God?

RLS

The garden was unending to the child
but Mr Hyde was there, behind each tree.
A high bright sun smiled down; the breeze was mild;
the garden was unending. To the child
the trees were masts. He sailed across the wild
South Seas until he reached his final quay.
His Eden seemed unending; he was beguiled;
and Mr Hyde was there, behind each tree.

A READING BY GEORGE BRUCE

(Fruitmarket Gallery, Edinburgh 25.01.1998)

You see? he said, and, yes, we did. He took
us to Temple for hot soup and sherry,
a chat about art with William Gillies.

An old man, a wee boy, he roved back and forth,
up and down the century. *The cliffs erode,
they erode,* he exclaimed, his eyes amazed.

Always the sea, shaping the stone, a kind
of art in itself, while his mother brought
the children a plate shining with herring;

while he argued the toss with MacDiarmid
and won. At times, behind his black lectern,
he was the dominie; we were the bairns.

He showed us how it was, is, and should be,
and accidentally dropped his watch. It lay
between his polished shoes, in danger

of being crushed. For a second he faltered
but quickly journeyed on; then, talking done,
scooped up the watch, intact, time still ticking;

time still to gather bright shells from the shore.

MR MACCAIG CAME TO STIRLING

(Central Library—January 1991)

I was the would-be entrepreneur; he,
without doubt, the star. Unfolding, he smoked
below my big *No Smoking* sign. Then,
dragging a leg, he faced his crowd. A joke

as dry as finest malt, then Mr MacCaig
was away, off through a world of short walks
that ended with long conclusions; then sheep
and stone; mortality; and trains. He talked

to us a complete hour, with measured words,
quick gleams and perfect pauses. In his streets
and hills, we saw with his eyes, knew Scotland
and eternity. He even stood to treat

us all with Hints About His Writing.
How long did he take to make a poem?
He answered well, but didn't tell. Some folk
called him Norman, as though they were at home

with an uncle or old pal. And the stags
stood quiet by the birch wood, while the white horse
bared its teeth at the wind. Later, I sped
through the night with Mr MacCaig. The view

from the train was ourselves: me, and his long head
smoking and talking, through Larbert, Falkirk,
Linlithgow. Until he started to sing
to me, as though he'd known me forever—

but Norman could sing for almost anyone.
The train rolled on; it slid into our station.
Shutters were shut; the clock's hands close to midnight;
but frosted pavements shone like constellations.

WALKING FOR CENTURIES

(A poem for Nigel Tranter)

He walks for miles in waxed coat, cap and breeches.
He follows a familiar route, twelve miles perhaps,
of dunes and bents, shining acres of unmarked sand.

With the keen east wind in his still-sharp eyes
he looks towards the Bass, where covenanters
shiver and die, ten thousand gannets scream.

Then he stops to note down a thought or two,
while the firth provides a rhythm, an eternal
punctuation. His chapter is unfolding.

Later, as the sun grows weak, he marches
westwards, seeing green Inchcolm, where canons
ponder manuscripts, drift silently to prayer.

He's been walking now for centuries, yet knows
a lifetime's work is very far from finished:
histories have no ends, and no beginnings.

At times the beaches teem with kings and queens—
and ordinary folk. He paces Scotland's edge
while searching deep into his country's heart.

ADELAIDE AT SARENAC*

With time to kill and winter near,
she created a new form of verse:
twenty-two syllables, five short lines.
Ideal to pass her hours away.

No point in starting something big;
one image really says it all.
Like the sudden white moth that flew
so close, as the short day darkened,

grew so cold. She sat on the porch
counting the weeks—and syllables:
two, then four, then six, then eight. Two
brought the brief surprising end.

Sunk in her robe, she wrote cinquains,
heard passing ghosts in brittle leaves.
Was she convinced that little was more,
there, with that spondee, slow TB?

* *The American poet, Adelaide Crapsey (1878-1914), invented
the cinquain form.*

ADELAIDE'S GARDEN

Her spade
descends and cuts
the earth and now the worm
that singularly slid through slime
is two.

Lichen
creeps green across
the leaning fence and takes
each board, slow, into the waiting
landscape.

POET

He had to go into a home: his words
were not enough to cope with life. He sat
and stared with silent men, as pipe-smoke hung,
and evening settled quietly down around them.

Until she came with her bagful of poems,
her therapeutic verses. *Now listen
to this and then we'll discuss.* Some life hung
in the afternoon; eyes reflected light.

Then one day something very special: *One
of my favourites!* she told the men, and words
spun up and down the walls and danced and cried
till he turned his head and announced to her

that he was the author of that poem: he'd
had those thoughts when he still had thoughts. She smiled
and said, *Of course you did.* So he improved;
he soon got out and set up home alone.

She visits him on Saturdays. He gives
her poems; she washes his clothes. And now
he's quite himself again, brimming with words,
but far too sad to make a cup of tea.

THE NEXT POEM

Watch as the moon moves slowly over
the distant domes of Sacré-Coeur,
and the skin on your face is like linen.

Feel in your palm the cool bloodless hand
of the pale Madonna who lost her faith;
she parts her lips for you alone.

Then go to one of those rooms in Paris,
high in the prow of a shiplike building,
your view an unending boulevard.

Close the dust-hung velvet drapes;
listen for breathing that is not yours,
and wait there for hours or forever.

The world might mutate, while your tongue
strains hard to articulate. Pray that words
will tumble out, the Seine will fill with stars.

IN THE LOUVRE

Some call me Aphrodite, but that's all
Greek to me. To friends, I'm simply Venus;
to be precise—de Milo. In this hall
I've stood near-naked for years; I'm seen as
quite a sexy thing, the way my gown slips
down. And, yes, my breasts are firm to the touch.
But don't you dare—I'm being watched. My lips
are cool, they wait to be kissed, and as such
have waited for centuries. If only
I could move from here. I've heard Apollo
stands tall in bronze (and looks a little lonely).
Slave boys cavort and Cupid too. All go,
or so it seems. I imagine their charms,
remember holding lovers in my arms.

STILL LIFE

(Giorgio Morandi speaks)

1964, and I'm here still,
painting my portraits of bottles and jars,
in umbers, creams and eau de Nil.

What, though, is time? Fifty years
are as five minutes, with countless
receptacles to rearrange, then paint,

in here, in my mother's apartment.
I'll edge the moon-coloured one to the right:
a change is as good as a holiday.

My sisters say I'm in need of a break:
Giorgio, they ask, *why not step out
and paint the vibrant streets, the teeming people*

*of Bologna? Go, now, to the hills;
capture the colour of wind in the pines,
follow the flight of the mountain eagle.*

I say, *No need.* And those who see
no evidence of progress in my work
don't know this ochre jar is nearly perfect,

perspectives eternally changing.
I pour my life into these bottles
but my art, like love, cannot be measured.

THOUGHTS OF DIEGO VELÁZQUEZ

(An Old Woman Cooking Eggs, 1618)

So, here I am, at just nineteen,
trying to make a name for myself;
yet those two there are hardly aware
of my painstaking toil, my presence.

She, so stoical, and self-contained,
must weary greatly, seated for hours
while I strain for the glaze of terracotta,
the cloudiness of albumen, spreading.

And he, dour boy, his thoughts elsewhere,
displays the melon and flask of glass.
I'll show Seville how well I paint—
bright brass and china, basketry, skin.

I highlight all against the dark:
utensils, woman, child, three eggs.
Lowly matter, some might decide
and really not the stuff of art.

But kitchen scenes are my beginning.
I will paint merchants, courtiers, kings.
Who knows, some day I might be famed
in every palace and hall in Spain.

INTÉRIEUR JAUNE ET BLEU

(Pompidou Centre, Paris)

Join me, quick, in my blue and yellow room
where the table and chair have wiggly legs
and the carpet has been autographed. Join
me for lunch: there's watermelon (mostly)
but, if you wish, four lemons as well. There's
strong yellow coffee to wash it all down
or, if you prefer, a cool greenish drink.
Later, the oil lamp can be lit. We'll watch
the sky, as squiggles of black slip away.
We'll slump by the blue rectangle, marvel
at six lemon leaves—so brilliantly,
unexpectedly green. You'll love my room;
you'll want to meet the designer. I call
him, simply, Henri: man of few colours,
fewer words. But an artist, *I* believe.

DEATH IN VENICE

Von Aschenbach thinks as the tide comes in,
This is not the Ganges delta. His lips
close round a strawberry. (It's such a sin,
that luscious, dead-ripe fruit.) He sees the hips,
the milky skin of Tadzio. That boy
is perfect classical grace: Greek ideal,
a thing one might aspire to. Oh, what joy
to wait, to watch. And is such beauty real?
In dark back streets, a hot wind stifles. Stone
is sluiced down with disinfectant. A man
is observed; he's powdered and rouged. Alone
he returns to the sand, refines his plan.
Close by his chair a tiger waits to spring.
The tide goes out, a woman starts to sing.

AT EDLINGHAM CHURCH, NORTHUMBRIA

At one of Christianity's cradles, mist
is thinning on the moors. Our early walk
is to the castle's broken walls, but first
we pass the church, a low grey place of rock.
And with the singing of the wind, a psalm
blends in with high birds calling. Words of praise
have risen here since Bede (exalting Rome)
grew blind while writing histories. March clouds
prohibit the sun. Chilled, we stand as still
as gravestones. The castle's tower leans, held
only by a new steel strut. Then voices tell
us worship's over. Folk file out; some nod.
A congregation numbering only five,
warmed by Calor gas, keeping God alive.

EAST NEUK

At Crail, Anstruther, Pittenweem,
the living's lean, the boats are few.
Days are empty as empty creels
at Crail, Anstruther, Pittenweem.
A sighing's in the grey-green sea
as men remember vanished crews.
At Crail, Anstruther, Pittenweem,
the living's lean, the boats are few.

THE WRECK

At this age when the heart can suddenly stop
should I have come so far alone?
The current's pull is very strong,

just six feet from the rusting hulk
and edges of rough-torn metal.
The water feels much colder here.

I cannot see you on the beach
because I've come so far alone.
Have you noticed I'm invisible?

I must get to the giant propeller;
I have to swim on round the stern
as the water feels much colder here.

Do you look up anxiously from your book
to see how far I've gone alone?
Is the sun's heat searing your shoulders?

I remember how, on the other side,
the sea waits, warm as your embrace—
but the water feels much colder here
at this age when the heart can suddenly stop.

FROM THE HILL

Crows cloud over the fading horizon;
they shriek at the rise of another moon.
Night, yet again, is about to take hold.
This landscape is an empty cradle.
And everywhere the loneliness of fields,
earth broken down to grey frozen lumps.
Hear, now, that scuttling in the undergrowth:
the unknown creature getting away.
There is no music in the wind,
just a cold irregular breathing,
cold as the stars that eat at my heart
as another November ceases to be.
And, over there, a string of light—
a train gliding on its single track,
silent, distant, and carrying strangers
all the way from where to wherever.
This irretrievable day dissolves.
Time to start down the path again,
hoping it's one that leads me home,
far from the hill, and her shadow.

WHAT THEY DID ON THEIR HOLIDAY

She squeezed the juice from half a lemon,
licked the drops from her fingertips;
he picked the biggest, pinkest prawn,
slit its shell from end to end.

Sunburn stung her arms and thighs—
too long lying on baking sand.
One star appeared beyond the hilltop;
its brightness pierced the darkening sky.

She cut a slice of soft goats' cheese,
bit into its salty whiteness.
Let's pay, he said, and chose an olive,
firm, and coloured like a bruise.

AN EVENING IN

Put on some Johnnie Ray, she says, and runs
her tongue along her lipstick. Ten past ten:
she feels like fun. The sparkling white wine grows
warm in her glass; and there, her fingerprints.
'Just Walking in the Rain', she says, and lights
one more last cigarette. Candles can make
things romantic, can't they? The shadows move.
Maybe she should close the curtains, stop folk
staring in. And why do those streetlamps have
haloes? Oh, God, she's in love, and has been
for years—the endless romance of it all!
She drinks more wine, surveys the room's expanse.
The teddy bears get ready for the dance.

IT'S MAGIC

On the rainiest day of September
we bury another dead aunt.

I spy Doris Day in the graveyard,
in an anorak and stout shoes.

I leave the grieving congregation
as Doris has planned a picnic for me:

Wagon Wheels and Cremola Foam
while the sun peeps through the cypresses.

She says, *It's been a long long time*,
and shows her perfect glittering teeth.

Too long, I say as I stiffly sit.
(I can just hear How Great Thou Art.)

Hey, how about a singsong? she grins.
Something to drive those blues away.

I think and it's 1958:
Hang down your head, Tom Dooley, I bawl,

hang down your head and cry;
hang down your head, Tom Dooley,

poor boy, you're bound to . . .
Stop, says Doris and packs the picnic away.

Black figures stand at the chapel door;
time for tea and thin-cut sandwiches.

It's the rainiest day of September:
time, I guess, to board that Deadwood Stage.

SNAPSHOTS

Startling
gestures and positions:
your washing in the wind.

Leaves and stalks,
withered, brown;
still, one firm green courgette.

Pointing to the moon,
the crooked arm
of the old oak tree.

On the carousel
the old suitcase
unclaimed again.

This lamplit A4.
Beyond here,
dark rooms.

STATIONS

I thought some day I might go to Minsk,
Sundsvall, Sottens, Allouis, Limoges,
and the dozen other faraway places
with strange-sounding names on the wireless.

We tended to stay with the Medium Wave:
Light Programme and Scottish Home Service.
But left alone I roamed the globe—
well over thirteen hundred metres.

I loved the way the dial lit up,
a friendly glow in a friendless night.
The valves grew warm as did the wood.
Can I please stay up for Luxembourg?

And suddenly I'm sixty and in the age
of communication; I keep my wireless,
which needs a dust. I peer at its dial,
wondering if I'll ever get to Minsk.

YEAR'S END

Give me any day in summer, and not
the year's bleak midnight. The radio tells
me we are older, have less time to share.
How I need you, and how I fear the bells.